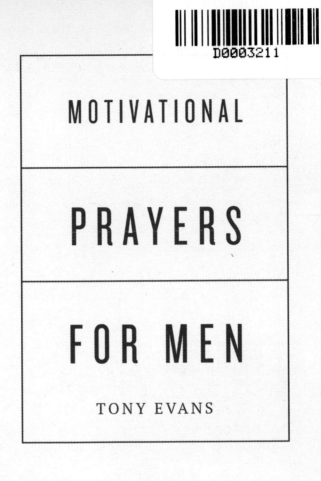

MOTIVATIONAL

PRAYERS

FOR MEN

TONY EVANS

HARVEST HOUSE PUBLISHERS
EUGENE, OREGON

Scripture quotations are taken from the New American Standard Bible®, © 1960, 1962, 1963, 1968, 1971, 1972, 1973, 1975, 1977, 1995 by The Lockman Foundation. Used by permission. (www.Lockman.org)

Cover by Brian Bobel Design

Cover photo © RNMitra / iStock

Motivational Prayers for Men
Copyright © 2019 by Tony Evans
Published by Harvest House Publishers
Eugene, Oregon 97408
www.harvesthousepublishers.com

ISBN 978-0-7369-7852-1 (pbk.)
ISBN 978-0-7369-8538-8 (eBook)

Library of Congress Cataloging-in-Publication Data is on file at the Library of Congress, Washington, DC

Printed in the United States of America

19 20 21 22 23 24 25 26 27 / VP-GL / 10 9 8 7 6 5 4 3 2 1

CONTENTS

1

A PRAYER FOR HEALTH

Lord, I want to thank You for giving me my life and my body. Thank You as well for giving me the tools to serve You through my physical well-being. I pray, Lord, that You would increase my wisdom so that I can guard this temple called my body and govern myself in a healthy way. Please ward off those things that would impede me from living a fully healthy life—not only for myself, but also for my family. Let my hands, feet, legs, limbs, mind, speech, hearing, sight, and all other components of my physical body be used by You for Your maximum glory.

I trust You, Father, to use my body and to keep

it strong so that I can serve You well and bring good to others. I know that when I am physically healthy, then I am better able to focus on my usefulness to You as well as to my family. I ask that You will both protect and help my family and loved ones in this area too; my desire is for them to be healthy.

Lord, You are the God who heals. If something does go wrong with regard to health in our home, would You intervene and give us insight so that we can have medical professionals help take corrective action? We are looking to You and You alone for our ultimate well-being. Thank You that You are the God who gives life, strength, and health to us. I trust You in Your ongoing care for me and my loved ones. In Christ, amen.

> "We need to realize that even though life is given to us, life is not due us; it is a gift."

2

A PRAYER FOR STRENGTH

Lord, Your Word says that when we are weak, we are actually strong. I want to be a strong man for You. I want to be the kind of man whom You can use in many ways to advance Your kingdom. I ask that You give me the strength to make the right choices in my personal spiritual walk and growth to maturity. Give me the strength as well to deal with the pressures that come to me each day. And help me to have the resolve to see all things through to completion.

Lord, I ask that You would enable me to rightly handle all my responsibilities, as well as the things that I don't expect to come my way. When issues and difficulties arise, may I face them well and with dignity. May I grab hold of them and walk through them in full dependence upon You, leading those under my care through those situations as well. I also ask for the wisdom to know when I should hold back from making a commitment, and instead, delegate it to someone else. In Christ, amen.

> "Many of God's men are spiritually anemic because Christ is not first in their lives."

A PRAYER FOR ACCESSING
THE POWER OF GOD

Lord, I ask for the wisdom to make decisions about the best way to move forward in my personal life, family life, and my work. Give me the courage and strength to go against the grain when it is right to do so. May I be willing to take a stand when the odds don't appear to be in my favor and yet I know it is You calling me and prodding me in a specific direction. Help me not to succumb to the devil's attempts to discourage me. Help me to rely on You in those times. You give strength to the weary, and Lord, sometimes I do feel worn out. I do feel weak. I do get tired to the point of wanting to give up or throw in the towel. That's when I need the extra strength You promise to those who look to You in a spirit of humility and dependence, like Isaiah 40 says—You renew those who wait on You and give them wings like eagles. When I want to quit, give me the resolve not to. Help me learn the art of relying on You so that I don't carry the burdens of life on my own.

I am looking to You for Your power and provision. You alone are my strength. If I'm going to make it in this life wrought with ongoing challenges, busy schedules, and unrelenting demands, it will only be because You enable me to do so. Lord, I thank You for all that is mine through You. By faith, I believe that You are providing what I need for each moment, each hour, and each day. In Christ, amen.

"Do you want to see God's power operating on your behalf? Become a man of integrity who refuses to make excuses."

A PRAYER FOR BECOMING A BETTER HUSBAND

Dear Lord, You have positioned me in such a way that I am to provide the spiritual covering for my wife. First, I want to thank You for entrusting me with this high calling, and for blessing me with my life partner. I wish to cover her with Your Word and with my love. Help me, Lord, to see to her overall well-being. Give me an understanding heart toward her needs and her desires. You have said in Scripture that husbands are called to understand their wives. I want to understand my beloved—and to do so more and more with each passing day. Help me to be willing to listen to her so that I can know her more fully and understand her personality, passions, and purpose for Your kingdom. I desire to care for her better and in so doing, to even predict or anticipate her needs so that she sees my care in advance of her stating what she wants.

Help me not to view my relationship with my wife from a selfish mindset, looking at her only in terms of what she can do for me. Rather, help me to find a way to offer something of benefit to her each and every day so that she sees I am thinking about her and contributing to her well-being even when it's not requested.

Father, I pray that You will enable me to comfort my wife when she needs comfort. Help me to encourage her when she needs encouragement. You have said I am to love her as Christ loves the church. I want to do that, Lord, but I need Your wisdom and Your Holy Spirit's guidance about how to do that with kindness and love. Thank You for giving me the privilege of doing that as her spiritual head and leader.

In Christ, amen.

> "A husband's love is meant to be so powerful that it transforms his wife into what she should be, just as Christ's love for the church transforms us into what we should be."

5

A PRAYER FOR MY CHILDREN

Lord, I pray for my children today and every day. I pray for each one individually as well as all of them collectively. I bring them before Your throne as Your own. They are Yours, Lord, and I have been placed over them as a leader, guide, father, and friend. I pray that You will protect them not only when they are in our presence in the home, but especially when they are away from home. Protect them not just from safety issues but also from the wrong kinds of people who may be giving them the wrong advice and taking them in the wrong direction. Let Your Holy Spirit remind them of the things that they have been taught so that they don't succumb to smooth-speaking people who mean them no good. Help us as parents to be preemptive in catching things that our children need to be warned of and to address those with compassionate leadership.

Lord, please protect our children while they are in school. I pray not only for their physical safety, but also that You will protect them from errant teachers and errant teaching that is designed to put them on the wrong path. Place a border of protection around their minds from certain ways of thinking that are contrary to Your Word and to what I am teaching them as a father and as a kingdom man.

Lord, I pray that when my children come of age, You will bring a godly marriage partner into their lives whom they can love and who will love them in return. I ask for future mates who will reinforce the Christian family heritage that we have sought to enforce in our own home. I also pray for my children's well-being, productivity, and opportunities, and that they will find Your purpose for their lives. Most of all, I pray that each child will not only come to Christ for salvation, but will also follow Jesus as a kingdom disciple. In Christ, amen.

"If we're going to fight a good fight for our kids, we need to get our own act together. Children don't mind following someone who's showing by example how it's done and who's doing it with them."

6

A PRAYER FOR STRENGTH OF CHARACTER

Lord, character matters—to You, to me, and to those under my care and in my sphere of influence. I desire to display godly character in my own life, but there have been times when I have not demonstrated the kinds of traits that a kingdom man should have. Lord, I want to do better. I want to reflect the character of Christ in my actions, my decision making, and my relationships.

Forgive me for the instances in which I have not shown godly character. Give me Your mercy for those times when my public and private lives have not been in cadence with each other. I am sorry for the times when my life has lied about what my lips were saying. Thank You, Lord, for Your grace and forgiveness. Help me to walk in bold confidence knowing that You desire me to do so, rather than to walk in shame from things I have done in the past. And give me strength of character moving forward. Grow me in this area of my life so that what I say is who I am, and what I portray publicly is what I am privately.

Lord, help me to be strong when I need to take a stand for what is right. I also want to be a good example for those who look to me as a role model. Let me live in such a way that I am someone worth following. Make me a man of high standards, a man who doesn't lower the bar simply because other men around me are doing so. Make me a man who can be trusted with truth and responsibilities. Help me to never let down my employer or employees; may I be known as someone who is reliable and dependable. May my words always be sure, like nails driven deeply into a wall. Make me that kind of man in both my workplace and my home. In Christ, amen.

> "When you are a man of integrity,
> God deals with your enemies for you."

7

A PRAYER FOR BEING THE HEAD OF THE HOME

Lord, I pray that You will enable me to uphold the role You have given me as the head of my home. I do not want to compromise my role due to passivity or external pressures. Rather, I want to be the man of the house in the way that You define manhood. I want to be able to say, with Joshua, "As for me and my house, we will serve the LORD" (Joshua 24:15). I don't want there to be any questions about whether I am fulfilling my biblical obligation as the head of this home. That means that I want to fully accept the responsibility of raising my children in the proper fear of God. I want to accept Your call to cover my family and to provide for them. Help me to be a good provider. I want to meet my wife and children's needs, and, as You enable me, to give them their wants as well—but to do so in a way that shows I am seeking their best interest.

Lord, as the head of my home, I desire to protect my family from hurt, harm, and danger. I want them to feel safer with me than with anyone else, and safe because of me. Help me to not bring harm to my family in any way, whether through how I speak to them, treat them, relate to them, or guide them. May my work not supplant them. May my phone or laptop not replace them. Let me be fully present with my family so that they know I take my role seriously. May my headship affirm that I am a loving husband and father, that I am a caring man— God's man for this home. And that our home will be governed by You through me so that everyone knows that You are running the show here. Lord, help me to be the man of the house You have called me to be because I want to be the kingdom man You have designated me to be. In Christ, amen.

> "Whenever a husband shifts the burden of leadership to his wife, he makes a serious mistake."

A PRAYER FOR WISDOM IN LEADERSHIP

Lord, I want to lead well. But to do that means that I need to be led by You first and foremost. I cannot lead based on my own understanding, or I will lead those in my care astray. Father, I want to lead according to Your will and Your Word. I need wisdom to do that. I need You to inform me about the way to apply Your will and Your Word in my various decisions in life.

I don't want to lead poorly by making bad decisions that not only jeopardize me but also those who are following me—starting with my family, and then others. Lord, let me not merely be a leader by title. I want to be a leader by my decisions, protection, guidance, and covering. Help me to determine not only what is okay or good, but what is best. To do so, I need Your help when I make decisions. May Your Holy Spirit inform my thinking and my emotions so that I make the best choices possible. And give me the will to follow through so that I am not just talking about what we ought to do as a family or at work, but that I am doing it myself and modeling it for others.

Lead me so that I can lead others well. Because if You don't lead me, I will lead poorly based on my imperfect humanity. I'll be leaning on myself, and that will not produce the results You desire for my life and in the lives of those I lead. Thank You, God, for answering this leadership prayer. In Christ, amen.

> "Position, power, and possessions don't last. What lasts is what is done in obedience to the King of kings and the ruler over all."

A PRAYER FOR FINANCIAL SECURITY

Father, You are my source. In fact, You are my only source. Help me not to inadvertently replace You by looking to an illegitimate resource. Help me not to put anything in Your place in order to meet my needs. May I look to You as my provider—it is You who provides an income, opens doors for job opportunities, and makes it possible to pay our bills. As the head of the family, I often feel like all these responsibilities rest on me, and the pressure can prove weighty. But there is freedom in knowing that while I must be responsible, ultimately, You are the One who provides. Help me to remember that everything we have is because You are supplying for us, and not because of what I am doing.

Thank You for Your provision. Thank You for meeting our needs. Thank You for food, clothing, and shelter—the essentials that are necessary for living in this world. Most of all, thank You for the peace that comes from knowing that You intimately care for us and will supply all our needs. With that in mind, may my heart seek after You and my life align under Your overarching rule.

My eyes are on You alone as my source—not my employer, and not my money. In the same way You provided for Elijah when he had no way to take care of himself, You give me what I need. Help me not to become preoccupied by what I lack because Your thoughts are higher than my own. Also, help me to be a good steward of the resources You have given to me and to those whom I love. Lord, grant me financial wisdom, and with it, financial security.

"God, in His grace, will supply whatever you lack so that He can get you where He wants you to go."

A PRAYER FOR FINANCIAL FREEDOM

Lord, would You help me to become financially free? You made it clear in Your Word that the borrower is a slave to the lender, and I don't want to be a slave to credit card companies, bills, or consumer debt. I don't even want to be a slave to my home mortgage. Help me to have the wisdom, insight, and personal discipline that are necessary to become financially free.

Father, guide me on how to use Your Word as the basis for my financial freedom. Show me how to not do foolish things with my finances, lest I come to You later asking for financial blessings in order to pay off the foolish choices I have made. Help me, instead, to be wise with all my financial decisions, whether large or small. Then, by Your mercy, help me to overcome the poor financial decisions of the past.

I'm asking you to set me free. Give me the wisdom and discipline to become financially free from debts and bills that will prevent me from giving generously and helping others. Lord, help me to trust You for financial freedom because You are my source. You are the provider of all that I have, and I look to You to help me grow in this area of my life. In Christ, amen.

> "There's nothing wrong with being rich. There's everything wrong with making riches your goal."

A PRAYER FOR HAPPINESS IN MY HOME

Dear Lord, may You make my home a place of happiness, peace, and joy. Would You help our family to be surrounded by an atmosphere of celebration? May the same be true about my work and any other area of my life—let happiness be known to accompany me there. You said that the joy of the Lord is our strength and that we should pursue peace with everyone. I want this to be the norm and not the exception. I want my home to be a place where I personally invoke joy, celebration, and fun with family members and friends. Help me to be a good steward of our dedicated family time so that we laugh together, celebrate together, and enjoy each other's company.

May I not forget to emphasize the important things in my family—the milestones and successes, the efforts put forth by each member even if the results don't accomplish the goal. May I be a strong and consistent cheerleader for my family so that our relationships are punctuated by peace and highlighted by happiness.

Keep me from discouraging my family, friends, and co-workers. Guard me against unbiblical anger, frustrations, and venting. May I not be inconsiderate with my time or my tongue. Rather, make wherever I am a fun place to be. Make my home an abode where happiness abounds because the joy of the Lord is within our walls from the front door to the back. I desire to hear my family members say that they love being with each other simply because of the environment and atmosphere that I have set. Thank You, Father, for Your Spirit, who reminds me to make my home a place of laughter and love. In Christ, amen.

"Did you know that from a biblical standpoint, fatherhood is the most critical role in the family? It is the father who is to be responsible for the children, not the mom."

A PRAYER FOR SEXUAL INTIMACY

Lord, I pray for the intimacy between myself and my wife to be blessed with all You are willing to give and do for us. The sharing of sexual intimacy is a spiritual act, so I seek You in prayer to cover us, provide for us, and enliven us sexually. Bless our bed and our bedroom, Lord. I want You to be involved in our love like You were with Solomon and his bride. I desire for this to be a special time as we share our love, our lives, and our bodies with each other.

Lord, help me to be attracted to and desire my wife only, and help my wife to be attracted to and desire me only. Give us eyes only for each other.

Awaken in us attraction and passion. Forgive me for any lust that I have had or do have in my heart. Remove any desires in me that take me away from the sexual loyalty I am to have with my bride, as well as her loyalty to me. Make our sexual relationship exciting, and make it the highest physical expression we share of our commitment to one another. May it give us the sense that a covenant is being renewed every time we are sexually intimate with each other. Because You created this wonderful and enjoyable activity, take us to the deepest level of sexual satisfaction and experience in our marriage. Let us know all that You have for us in this area of our lives so that we can fully experience all we have been endowed to feel by You. Bond us together so much that we mutually crave each other on a regular basis. Give us wisdom and insight on how to please each other on a greater level as well. In Christ, amen.

> "I often tell husbands to quit being so boring, so predictable. Remember how spontaneous you were when you dated your wife?

You were always doing the unexpected, springing little surprises on her. Now you say, 'Where do you want to go tonight?' That's not very creative."

A PRAYER FOR ENJOYING LIFE

Lord, You've given us permission to enjoy life. Sometimes that's hard to do. Sometimes I feel that to allow myself personal pleasures doesn't seem very spiritual. Yet when You created the first man, Adam, You told him to enjoy the garden and that he could freely eat of every tree but one. You said this before You created Eve. Basically, You told Adam to take pleasure in Your provision. In fact, not only did You tell him to do that, but You commanded him to!

Lord, help me to be truly okay with having fun. Help me to truly delight in the life You have given to me and for encouraging that enjoyment in my family and at work. Help me to see that You like to take pleasure in what You created. You said that every good and perfect gift comes from above (James 1:17). First Timothy 6:17 says that You have richly supplied us with all things to enjoy. And yet even though You have told us these things, we still fail to link *fun* and *God* together. Help me to see that You want to have fun with me, and You want me to have fun with You.

Sometimes it feels awkward to pray for more fun, but God, I want to delight in what You've given me permission to enjoy, and I want to do so to the max. Because, Lord, You enjoy pleasure. You've even asked me to live for Your pleasure. Help me to enjoy what You enjoy so that we can rejoice in it together. In Christ, amen.

> "If you're working so hard that you never get time with God or with your loved ones, you're working too hard. Your work was never meant to replace God in your life."

A PRAYER FOR MY FRIENDSHIPS

Lord, will You connect me with other men so that we can encourage each other to be stronger kingdom men? Guide me toward those friendships in life that are authentic and based on each of us truly desiring to be the men you have called us to be. Connect me with other men who exercise responsibility under You, live in relationship with You, and seek to interact in community with one another. Develop friendships in which I can communicate freely to others, and they to me.

Lord, give me a group of men in my church with whom I can relate on a spiritual level as well as in other ways outside of our church. May we become iron that sharpens iron, growing in You together. Because I know I cannot be a successful as a lone ranger Christian, I want to be a fully engaged saint with other godly men. Draw me into friendships with men of courage, character, commitment, and decency.

Father, give me a brotherhood. And make me a contributing member to this brotherhood. In Christ, amen.

"Good relationships are not just nice; they are biblically necessary."

15

A PRAYER FOR MENTAL CLARITY

Lord, it's been said that a mind is a terrible thing to waste, and oftentimes we are guilty of doing that because we are not thinking on the things You tell us to dwell on. I know my mind can wander quite frequently. You promise that as I let my requests be made known to you, Your peace will guard and guide my mind (Philippians 4:7). It will act as a garrison that protects my thoughts. Remind me that as I seek You, I will experience the calm that comes from You alone.

Please remove the chaos from my mind so that I don't live in mental torment and conflict, but rather, in mental harmony and peace. May the rest that You offer enable me to think clearly and to make right decisions. I realize that as I think good thoughts, they, in turn, will lead me to good actions. That shows all the more why I need to keep my attention focused on You!

Lord, give me the rest that the mind of Christ had as He walked on earth so that I'm thinking like He did. Your Word says that You give peace even when there is trouble. Christ is my example of calm in the middle of the storms of life. May Your peace that surpasses understanding be very real as I persevere through life's difficulties. I give my mind to You so that You may guard it. In Christ, amen.

> "Why does God want our minds? Because that is where the decisions of life are made. If we are going to be committed to Christ, He must have control of our minds."

16

A PRAYER FOR GREATER FAITH

Lord, will You grow my faith? I want to be a man who trusts deeply in You. I don't want to be a man of little or mediocre faith. I want to have awesome faith—a faith that believes You fully, follows You completely, and takes You at Your word. I want to be the kind of man whose belief shows up in my feet and not just my feelings. I want my whole life to reflect my faith, rather than just my lips. Help me to live as a man who acts like You are telling the truth even when I don't understand what You are saying or the path You've asked me to take. Increase my faith!

God, I want to believe You at such a level that

when I operate by faith I get to see You, experience You, and know You more fully. Lord, give me You. Give me You so much that my faith grows as I trust in You. Expand my faith and strengthen it. Yes, I know that means You may bring circumstances into my life that force me to trust You. But I know You won't give me more than I can handle. You'll place me in situations that are meant for my good and that will develop me into a man of faith. I don't want to hear You say to me, "O ye of little faith." I want to hear You say that You are proud of me because my faith is strong—because I choose to believe the great God who loves me and gave Himself for me even when I don't understand the way He leads me. In Christ, amen.

"You can't exercise faith in your easy chair."

17

A PRAYER FOR HELP IN NOT PROCRASTINATING

Lord, help me to get rid of my procrastination. Help me to start where I am right now and not wait for You to do something else before I get started. You tell me throughout the Bible that people had to act first before You acted because You wanted to see their faith in motion. Help me to do the same and to take the first step toward showing You that I believe You. Even if it is a small step, may it be a clear and obedient step—a step that You can see, honor, and expand upon.

Lord, help me to get rid of my excuses for why I can't obey You or do what You've told me to do. I'm so sorry for my procrastination, which hinders my blessing and hinders Your spiritual movement in my life. Help me to choose to follow the Lord Jesus Christ and the Holy Spirit in obedience to Your Word. Again, help me to take that first step. I may also need Your help with steps two, three, four, and five, but help me as I get started. Enable me to give You something to work with so that at least You see I'm not just talking but I am also walking—that I am taking seriously my walk of faith with You. In Christ, amen.

> "God is not going to force your victory on you. You have to go get it."

18

A PRAYER FOR TIME WITH GOD

Lord, one way I procrastinate too frequently is when it comes to spending time with You. I seem to be able to make time for myself pretty well. I've been good at setting aside time for the stuff I like to do, like watching sports or doing my favorite hobbies. I make time for work, watching the news, or surfing the Internet. Yet somehow I'm too busy—or too lazy—to make time for You. I confess that as a sin. Please forgive me.

I want to set a daily habit of making time for You—time in Your Word, time in Your presence, and time in prayer. I can't keep saying that I am unable to live without You yet go through my days living without You. So, Lord, I want Your Holy Spirit to wear me out with conviction when I miss my time with You while I'm making time for everything else. Here I am. I want to start today and no longer procrastinate—even if it's only five minutes, ten minutes, or fifteen minutes. Whatever it is, I want to start now.

You say in John 15 that without You, I can do nothing. I now choose to operate on that truth. I choose to give You time each day because You give me time *all* day every day. May I constantly be reminded that I cannot live this life without You. Correct me when I miss my appointment with You. And as time goes on, encourage me to increase it. I love You so much that I don't want to miss it anymore. In Christ, amen.

> "Make spending time with God the rule,
> not the exception."

19

A PRAYER FOR THE DINNER TABLE

Lord, You told me that the most precious time I have—according to Psalm 128:3—is with my family at the table. Lord, help me to make the most of that. Guide me on how to use the table as an opportunity to have a spiritual impact on my family. Let me use this occasion not only to eat but also to lead, bless, encourage, and guide my family in devotions—a time to fulfill my role as the head of the house, and that our house is under God.

Will You show me what to do at the table? Will You direct me on what devotions to read, prayers to lift up, and conversations to have? Please remove any distractions that would take us away from focused time on family and You. Take away those things that prevent us from maximizing this opportunity for spiritual and relational development. Lord, may I be present at the table as much as possible. And when I can't be available due to schedules or travel, may I give my family ideas for things they can do without me there.

Help me to communicate to my family the importance of the table, and help me to demonstrate it as much as possible. May my table time with them be our table time with You as a family. May everyone in our family come to view that time like no other. And may it impress upon my wife and children that I am serious when I say that in my house, we will serve the Lord. In Christ, amen.

> "A lot of us are trying to fix our wives or our children when God wants to fix us first."

20

A PRAYER FOR A GREATER CALLING

Lord, help me to accomplish great things for You. Give me something BIG to do for You. Let it be larger than my own capacity to pull off. And by big I'm not just talking about the size of it; I'm also talking about how You view it. Give me a calling that requires faith to do it well. Give me a responsibility that will truly matter for Your kingdom—that will matter for the salvation of souls, the discipleship of others, and the good of others.

Lord, give me a Goliath to slay, an enemy to conquer, a battle to be won. Give me a challenge—You created men to take on challenges! But I don't want to face a challenge without You. As Moses said, if You're not going into this challenge or battle with me, then I don't want to go. I want You more than the challenge itself, and I know I cannot win it on my own. I want to go, but not by myself. I want to go with You, and I do want that challenge. I want a kingdom assignment, Lord. I want something that will blow my mind, advance Your kingdom, impact the lives of people, and grow me spiritually.

God, give me a beast of a challenge so that You can take the manhood that You've given me and build it up. Give it to me, Lord; I want it. I'll take it. I'll receive it. I'll ask for it. But I don't want it without You alongside me. In Christ, amen.

> "You will often know that it is God asking you to do something if it is something you cannot do on your own."

21

A PRAYER FOR SEEKING GOD

Lord, may Galatians 2:20 define me. May You give me my identity in You. You told me that my identity is to be in Christ. You have made it clear that I'm to be identified first and foremost as a Christ follower. Help me to never substitute following Christ for following people. When I'm having to make a choice between identifying with You or with others, would You convict me toward choosing You only? Everything else must be second if it is to be there at all.

May I be a man who truly seeks first Your kingdom and Your righteousness. May Your standard be mine. May I not dumb down Your standard so that I can gain the acceptance of people around me. May I be willing to suffer with Christ because that is part of my identity in Him. If I've been rejected, may I gladly take up my cross because I've been accepted by You. And may I accept the consequences of that identity. May popularity with this world never trump popularity with You. May I remember that to love the world is to lose the love of the Father. It is to lose the experience of You at work in my life. May I not make the mistake of choosing this world over You. May I love You with my whole heart and embrace my identity in You more than anything else. In Christ, amen.

> "If you know God, you will know your purpose. Not because you went purpose hunting, but because you went God hunting."

22

A PRAYER FOR FREEDOM FROM TEMPTATION

Lord, You said that when it comes to temptation, You will not allow me to run into anything that I cannot handle. You said that there is no temptation for me but that which is common to man. Which means that when I am tempted, I am not alone—others have faced the same struggle too. And You promised that if I seek Your help, You will give me the ability to resist. I'm seeking You now, Lord, to not let Satan or circumstances bring anything into my life that is too big for me to deal with.

Lord, help me to handle temptation well. Help me to walk away from it—to have victory over or through it, however it comes. I also ask that You keep Satan from defeating me in those areas where I've been defeated in the past. Give me the road to recovery, a comeback, a reversal. So that even though for a moment I might be losing, I will end up winning because You've given me victory.

Give me what You gave Peter after he betrayed Jesus. Peter was too proud, and You humbled him, but then You gave him a path to recovery. I need a recovery, Lord. I need to recover my thoughts, actions, relationships, and family. Help me to over-rule temptation so that temptation is no longer able to overrule me. In Christ, amen.

> "Set your standards in advance. Decide your boundaries now so you don't compromise them when you find yourself in the middle of a problem."

23

PRAYER FOR CLOSENESS IN MARRIAGE

Lord, will You draw me closer to my wife? Will You make us one as a couple? There are a lot of things that divide us. We are different in our personalities and our desires. We have different goals. The children can also divide us. The same is true about our schedules. In fact, divisions exist all over the place, and they can hinder our relational intimacy. As a result, we end up experiencing times when we're not that close to each other anymore. When we don't want to talk to each other. Or we don't want to be around each other.

Lord, will You close that gap? Will You draw us back together and give us insight on how to guard ourselves and our relationship from the divisions that can make us drift apart?

Will You give me the wisdom to lead in this area of our marriage? Help me to close the gap when intimacy is lacking. May I summon the courage to let her know that we need to be closer, and that I'm willing to lead the way toward that because it is my responsibility. Draw us nearer together and remove the walls that have been built up over the days and years gone by. And bring harmony where there was once division.

Also, so that my prayers are not hindered according to 1 Peter 3:7, keep me mindful not to treat my wife with dishonor, or in ways that cause her not to feel equal. Draw me nearer to my wife each day, and draw us both nearer to You. In Christ, amen.

> "True love, *agape* love, does what is needed for the person loved whether or not the one doing the loving receives anything in return."

24

PRAYER FOR FREEDOM FROM BONDAGE

Lord, please give me the ability to identify and overcome the habits in my life that are not consistent with Your character. May I seek to be rid of any addictions or bondages through the power of Your might. I choose to break free of them. You have said that the bondage of Egypt ought not to be my bondage—that whom the Son sets free is free indeed. I give You permission to set me free, Lord. I urge You to do so. Please unlock my prison and let me walk out.

Lord, I ask Your intervention for any addictions or habits in my life that are outside of Your will and that hold me captive in my thoughts and actions. I don't want to be bound anymore. Instead, I want the one who owns me and makes me a slave to You. Please take off the shackles and set me free from wicked thoughts, actions, people, relationships, schedules, and anything else that is holding me captive. For everything holding me hostage, Lord, I give You permission to break it. I want to be freed from life's traps so that I can walk in victory. In Christ, amen.

> "My prayer is that God will use His Word to help Christian men today avoid the degrading, destructive trap of sexual sin. And the best place to avoid this destructive trap is on the front end, when sin is not yet conceived—and we call that a temptation."

25

A PRAYER FOR FORGIVENESS

Lord, may I release those whom I need to forgive. May I let them go from the debt I believe they owe me because of what they did to me. Give me the courage of Joseph, who was able to discern that the evil his brothers did to him was allowed by Your hand for the ultimate good of many. Help me to see that the wickedness done against me had to pass through Your fingers first. It didn't get to me without coming through You for a reason that You intended. Because I trust You, I can also forgive those around me.

And where there is repentance by the other person, give me the willingness to bring about reconciliation.

Even if he doesn't ask for forgiveness, may I choose to forgive so I can be set free. But in the times when a person genuinely seeks forgiveness, may I be willing to rebuild that which was torn down or lost. Give me the grace of a forgiving spirit so that I don't burn a bridge I may need to cross myself. Remind me of the need to cross the bridge of forgiveness with You on a regular basis, as well as with others. And help me to offer forgiveness to others because I need it for myself. Help me to go to those from whom I need forgiveness as well and ask it of them. In all cases, let me live in peace with everyone—as much as it is possible to do so. In Christ, amen.

> "If you are a Christian, you not only belong to God because He created you, you belong to Him because He redeemed you."

26

A PRAYER FOR RUNNING MY RACE WELL

Lord, may I be a man who runs after You. I want to choose You in every moment and every day of my life. May I chase whatever greatness You have for me—not just think about it, but pursue it diligently. I want to end my race in this life the same way Paul ended his. He said he fought a good fight and kept the faith. He finished the course, and he left this place with fire in his bones. I want fire in my bones too. I want the man in me to be a flame when I leave this earth because I pursued God's definition of greatness for me.

For me, greatness and success can be defined as having done the work You gave me to do. Having finished the race You gave me to run. Lord, don't let me leave the track before I finish. Don't let me depart early, before it is all done. If anything, may I pick up the pace so that I can make up for lost time. I don't want to fall behind any further. I don't want to lose any more energy. I don't want to lessen my effort.

Father, make me Your man. Make. Me. Your. Man. Make me end this race strong, with greatness. Help me to hear what Stephen heard when he left this earth. He saw You stand up for him. He got a standing ovation. He received Your Spirit. Oh Lord, that's what I want—to end this race well, cross the finish line, and hear you say, "Well done, My good and faithful servant."

> "If you are going to be a part of Jesus's kingdom and carry out the kingdom agenda, you have to meet His demands."

27

A PRAYER FOR GROWING WITH GOD'S WORD

Lord, as I sit before Your Word and meditate on what You have said, I ask that Your Holy Spirit give me understanding. As I sit before Your truths, I ask that You help me understand what the author of the text is saying to his audience, and also what You are saying to me. Give me insight to know what You're telling me to do. Open my mind so that I know what You want me to think and where You want me to go. Please speak to me from Your Word and Your Spirit, and give me the power to apply what I read, learn, and study.

Don't let me go to church, hear the preacher, and

call it a day. Help me to be alert to Your Word and know what I should do. And keep me from procrastinating so that I follow through on Your instructions. May I not only be a hearer of the Word, but an effectual doer of it as well. You said that if I applied Your Word to my life, I would be blessed. With that in mind, I want to sit before it. I want to understand it. Then I want to do it so that I can get the benefits of obedience operating in my life. May I not neglect Your Word because that would be tantamount to neglecting You. Let the Holy Spirit speak to me from Your Word so that it influences my life and the lives I touch.

Lord, give me a love for Scripture. Make me a man who continually pursues and grows in the Word. Give me the discipline to not hurry when I sit before You. I don't want to merely "read a verse a day to keep the devil away." Rather, I want Your Word to be a primary focus in my life. Please bring scriptures to my mind by the power of Your Holy Spirit, and may I meditate on them and see them at work in my life. In Christ, amen.

"Don't merge what God says with what your friends say or with what you hear on the television or even with what you think."

28

A PRAYER FOR USING MY WORDS WISELY

Lord, guard my speech. May I honor You with the words that I say. May the words of my mouth and the meditations of my heart be acceptable to You. Govern what I say and how I say it. You've said that the tongue has the power of life and death. May I speak life. May I speak words of grace. According to Ephesians 4:29, may I not have speech that tears down, but instead, builds up.

Because words are expressions of my thoughts, please give me the right thoughts as I attempt to express the right words. Merge my thinking and my speech together so that the thoughts I think and the words I say become the words that the Holy Spirit wants said at any given moment. I desire Spirit-controlled thoughts and Spirit-controlled speech because 1 Corinthians 2:13-16 says that the Spirit wants to give me thoughts and speech out of the mind of Christ. I welcome both. Lord, make me a kingdom man in both my thoughts and my words. In Christ, amen.

> "The man who lives with integrity at home and in the marketplace will always stand out."

29

A PRAYER FOR BECOMING A LEADER

Lord, I don't want to simply lead and be known as a leader. Rather, I want to lead well. I want to be a quality leader—at home, at work, at church, and in my community. I don't want to be mediocre. I don't want to just get by. I want to excel and be the kind of man who has a lasting impact everywhere I go.

You call men to lead, and I want to fulfill that calling. I want to be a man who leads well in every sphere of influence that You place me. I don't want to lead outside of what You have entrusted to me; I want to do a great job within whatever realm You've called me to.

As I lead, correct me when I'm wrong. Give me training where I need it. Give me models and mentors who can help me brush up on my weak areas. Give me examples of great leadership in what I read, see, and experience. Please give me the Holy Spirit's wisdom so that I can lead in the way You desire for me to. I want those who are under my tutelage to know that they are going to be well because I'm leading well.

Help me to know how to best use the gifts of others so that they too can have a powerful impact in their spheres of influence. In all that I do as a leader, may I bring honor and glory to You. In Christ's name, amen.

> "God did not save you so you could become like everybody else. God saved you to be extraordinary."

30

A PRAYER FOR BECOMING A MENTOR

Lord, You've called me to not only be Your disciple but to also be a discipler of others. Show me who You want me to mentor. Show me which men, which young people You want me to influence to become kingdom men who will grow and follow me as I follow Christ. Show me those whom You want me to influence, those who would be responsive to my guidance. May I not only be following someone else's example, but may I also be an example to others. Yes, Lord, I want to be a mentor and influencer.

Help me to have a dynamic influence on the lives of others. I want them to be the people that You want them to be. May I have full dependence on the guidance of Your Holy Spirit so that I am a man who truly makes a difference. I want to be like Philip, who found Nathaniel, or Andrew, who found Philip. May I always be on the lookout for others whom I can influence. Help me to find people whom I can bring to You and grow in the faith. I want that for Your sake. In Christ, amen.

"God hits a moving target. Just like a quarterback would never throw to a man still standing on the line after the play was called, God is waiting on you to run your route. He will either increase or limit what He does in response to what you do."

31

A PRAYER FOR VICTORY OVER FEAR

Lord, as a man I often hide my fears. I cover them up so that others don't see them. I don't want people to think I'm fearful. So I keep my fears close to my chest. But the truth is I can't hide them from You. You know my heart and my concerns. You know what makes me anxious. So I want to tell You now the things that weigh upon my heart in the hopes that You can provide insights from Your Word that will bring me calm and assurance.

Sometimes I think about death, and it scares me. Especially when I hear about it in the lives of others. Or I become afraid when I hear about illnesses that other people have because I wonder what would happen if I or a loved one were to become similarly ill. Or I think about what could happen to my children. Sometimes I imagine the worst possible scenarios, which, in turn, cause me to worry. Even though you call worry a sin, I admit I succumb to it and I'm sorry. Forgive me.

I want to release and tell my fears to You. I want to tell You the truth about the things I'm scared of, the things I worry about, the things that cause me consternation. Lord, I want You to know my fears because I want You to guard me. I want to be honest with You in prayer and hand my fears over to You, whatever they might be. Sometimes I get scared about what's happening in our country. I get worried about what could happen to the people I care about. I get anxious about my sins.

Father, I invite You to invade my fears and turn them into faith. You do not want me to live in a spirit of fear, and I don't want fear to control me. I want to release my fears to You so that I can live in peace and confidence no matter what comes my way. In Christ, amen.

"God has as many methods
of fixing things as there are
stars in the sky. He is the great
unfigureoutable God."

32

A PRAYER FOR EMBRACING HOPE

Lord, You give hope. I love Jeremiah 29:11, which tells me that You have a plan for me, and that it is a plan for my well-being and not for my calamity. It is a plan to give me a future and hope. Lord, happiness isn't hope. I want the blessedness of hope. In Jeremiah 29, we read about how the people of Israel had made some serious mistakes and put themselves in a bad situation. Yet You still offered them hope.

Will You give me hope? Hope is future-oriented. Will You let me see that You haven't forgotten me as I pursue You? Will You let me find my way to You and restore my fortunes, including my emotional fortunes, such as peace and calm? As You said in Jeremiah 29:14, You can restore what I've lost. Lord, give me back the things that I've messed up, that I've sacrificed because of my sin. Give me hope for a better future for me and for the ones whom I love.

Lord, I'm sorry for the messes I've created. Give me the hope I need to help me overcome bondages I've succumbed to. Give me another chance to please You and to live for You, to love You and to be the kingdom man You created me to be.

Lord, give me hope, and with that hope may I honor You, seek You, serve You, and obey You. Allow me to maximize my manhood for Your kingdom. I want to be a kingdom man and not an ordinary one. Would You give me the hope that is a destiny that I can pursue? I want to run hot after You. I want to draw near to You as You have drawn near to me. In Christ, amen.

> "Sometimes God must lead you downhill so He can take you uphill."

33

A PRAYER FOR MY PASTOR

Lord, I pray that You will keep my pastor strong. Please keep him vibrant in Your Word. And keep him close to You so that he can lead me and other men to be the kind of men that we're supposed to be. Strengthen my pastor and give him rest of mind and heart as well as the ability to endure as he deals with the many burdens of ministry. Help him not to become discouraged. Show me how to encourage my pastor so that he's not feeling alone. May I be sensitive to the many demands on his time so that I don't end up preventing him from serving others in the congregation.

Father, I pray that my pastor would remain invigorated and that he will not succumb to the pressures and stresses of ministry. Guard him from the struggles and loneliness that often come with being in a leadership position. Keep my pastor's family strong; may his work in ministry not rob him of his home life. Create a positive home culture for him and his family so they don't develop a negative view of ministry. Cover my pastor fully, and may I never lose sight of the need to pray regularly for him and his well-being. In Christ, amen.

"Heaven will be at the disposal of those who are dependent on God. They are the ones who get their prayers answered, who see God intervene in life's circumstances, and who enjoy their Christian walk."

34

A PRAYER FOR SEEKING GOD

Dear Lord, make me a kingdom man. Not just a male, but the kind of man seen in Exodus 34:23-24, one who clearly places himself under the rule of God. May I place myself under Your divine authority so that I am operating under Your rule. Lord, help me to understand that You're in charge of me. Help me to embrace the reality that You want to have the final say-so over my decision making. I understand that You want to direct what I do, where I go, how I think, and what I say.

Help me to be a man of the kingdom. Help me to put You first, to seek first Your kingdom and Your righteousness. And help me not to seek my own kingdom, brand, platform, or profiles. May anything that I want to do come under Your rule and authority so that I'm operating according to Your guidelines. In Christ, amen.

> "Jesus took everything there is to know about God and put it on a shelf that we could reach. He is the complete revelation of God Himself."

35

A PRAYER FOR MY CHURCH

Lord, I ask that You bless my church, cover it, strengthen it, and give favor to it. May my church be the kind of place where men can come together and grow. Will You guide us in such a way that we will become a disciple-making church? And equip me so that I can serve as a contributor to that discipleship?

Lord, enable my church to raise men up to spiritual maturity and for me to be involved in that process. I ask that You set a plan in place that will result in the strengthening of the men there. Help me to become a mentor who knows how to live as an example to others. Give me opportunities to disciple men and make a difference not only in their lives, but the lives of all whom they know. May the ministry that I perform benefit the church and help people grow spiritually. May I meet the needs of those whom I serve, and remember to pray for those who serve with me. Together, may we become a vibrant force for good in our church.

Help our church to have an impact on our community. May we not just fulfill our duties, but have a ministry mindset about all we do, however big or small. Thank You for the fact that serving You brings personal reward and satisfaction, and that it changes lives. May I never simply go through the motions of carrying out a responsibility or assignment simply so I can check a box on my to-do list. I want everything I do to come from my heart. Lord, please cover the ministry in which I serve, and cover those who minister with me. Through it all, may Your name be glorified. In Christ, amen.

> "The test of our stewardship is whether
> God winds up with our leftover time,

energy, and resources, or we give Him our first and best. To put it another way, Jesus is either Lord of all, or He is not Lord at all."

36

A PRAYER FOR A SERVANT'S HEART

Lord, I pray that You would give me the heart of a servant. May I not become so independent or prideful that I want to be served and wind up not serving anyone else. Help me to be like Jesus, who sought to serve all. I want to be the kind of man who is willing to put on a towel, fill up a basin with water, and wash people's feet. Help me to understand what washing feet translates into for everyday life in today's culture. Give me opportunities to do this well, and provide the boldness and confidence I need to walk through the open doors You provide as I wash the feet of others. May I be a foot-washing kind of man, one who humbly serves.

Lord, I pray that You would equip and enable me to fulfill the destiny You've created for me to carry out. Help me to serve You in word and deed, and to glorify Your name in everything I do. To serve and honor You, Lord, is my highest purpose and goal. You are worthy of my service, commitment, love, time, and attention. May I give of my time, talents, and treasures as if doing so were second nature to me. In Christ, amen.

> "Realize the truth of the old saying that the best way to make a friend is to be a friend. Work hard at affirming others."

37

A PRAYER FOR BECOMING A MAN OF INFLUENCE

Lord, I want to be a man of influence. I want to make a difference, but I need to know how to do it. I need to know how and where You need me to serve. I want to be a man who moves other people in the right direction, which means I've got to move that way myself. So help me to be influenced by Your Spirit, which, in turn, will empower me to influence others. I want to be like Abraham, who had an impact on all the men who worked under him (see Exodus 8:17), including his own children. He was a man of influence who was accessible. Ultimately, his influence would bring about a national movement.

Make me a man of influence who helps stir movements among people. Or lead me so that I'm part of a movement that brings change. Lord, I don't want to merely live; I want to be fully alive in all I do. I want the life that You have given to me to flow through me so that others are motivated to seek You. Make me a model of doing right and being right so that others want to be more like You too. Make me a man whose presence here on earth is felt for Your glory, my growth, and the good of others. Help me to be a man of influence. In Christ, amen.

> "If we let the world's philosophy of male independence dominate us, we are courting spiritual, personal, and family disaster. It is critical that we learn to build relationships."

38

A PRAYER FOR LEAVING A LEGACY

Lord, help me to build a legacy. You say in Proverbs 13:22 that a good man leaves an inheritance for his children's children. He builds a legacy not just financially but emotionally and spiritually. I want to be like Asher, who had generations that followed after him doing the good he established for them to do. I want a legacy that outlives me, a legacy of a great reputation.

Lord, my heart's desire is for generations to be able to look back at my name and say that I walked with You, knew You, loved You, served You, and made a difference for You. Help me to build that legacy. Forgive me for when and where I've hurt that legacy or have not lived up to what You've given me to do. May I move forward from this point on with a renewed commitment. May I intentionally be future-oriented in my thinking and actions, and not just live in this moment. May I look ahead with a tomorrow mentality, a mindset that enables me to make a difference today because I'm thinking about the next day, and the next. I pray that my children will be blessed, and my children's children as well because of the legacy I leave behind. I pray this, Father, in the name of Your Son. In Christ, amen.

> "Every man must ask this question: What has God called me to do that is bigger than me?"

39

A PRAYER FOR AN ETERNAL PERSPECTIVE

Lord, give me an eternal perspective. Help me to see eternity and not just stare at time. May I live in time better and more productively because I see eternity more clearly. Help me to dream for heaven so that I live better on earth. Help me to see the reward of the judgment seat of Christ as a motivation for my decision-making now. Help me to reverse trends in my life that would take away the reward that You have for me so that I can stand before You with confidence. I do not want to be ashamed at Your coming because I squandered my days and my life.

Help me to live in light of Your coming, with an eternal perspective that spurs me to make good decisions and wise choices. It is true that You could come at any moment. Because of this, I want my moments to matter. I want Your will to be achieved because I'm looking at You. May my focus always be on heaven, mindful of the rewards You promise to give me in eternity based on my service to You on earth. Lord, help me to build my life not on wood and stubble but rather on gold, silver, and precious stones—all because I've embraced an eternal perspective. In Christ, amen.

"God has put within each one of us a sense of the eternal, a yearning for the things that are beyond space and time, things like ultimate purpose and meaning."

40

A PRAYER FOR EXERCISING SPIRITUAL AUTHORITY

Lord, I want to exercise legitimate authority in my life and in all the decisions that I make. I want to be able to call heaven's power and involvement down into the world in which I now live. Make me a prayer warrior who exercises binding and loosing under Your hand. Father, the authority that You have given to the church is the same authority that You have given to me. Make my intimacy with You to be so strong that John 15 is my legacy—that whatever I ask for, You answer because I'm so in touch with You that we're on the same wavelength and my prayers are heard by You.

Father, give me increased opportunities to exercise spiritual authority. May people see that I have the spirit of Elijah, and that Elijah's authority is on me. May the mantle that I'm carrying when I step into a room, when I'm involved with people, be Your mantle. May others sense God all over me. May they sense the anointing of Your Spirit. Lord, give me biblical authority so that I can bring change to people's lives because of the change You're bringing to my life and because Your Spirit is covering me. Endow me with Your Spirit's power, Lord, so that I can bring about changes for Your good and for Your glory, and for the benefit of others. In Christ, amen.

> "While God has set us among the routines of life, He wants us to look beyond the things of earth for something greater."

41

A PRAYER FOR THE SPIRIT'S LEADING

Lord, help me to hear the voice of the Holy Spirit so that I know when You are speaking to me. Train my ears to be able to hear what You are saying to me. I want to know that I'm not hearing foreign voices or being tricked by the devil. Cover me with the blood of Jesus Christ and protect me from Satan's twisting of Your Word or distorting of what is said to me by You. Give me spiritual sensitivity to You. Give me the anointing. Soften that receiver in my heart, mind, and spirit that picks up on the divine wavelength.

Lord, I want Your Spirit to speak into my human spirit so that my soul is fed by You. So that my mind is trained by You. So that my decisions are influenced by You. Will You give me an awareness of Your presence? Give me that inner sense, that inner radar that enables me to know how I am to act in whatever situation I am in. May the living Word penetrate the division of my soul and spirit so that I know what is of my thoughts and what is of Your thoughts. Help me to make my choices and decisions from Your divine perspective, not my human one.

Lord, speak to me. I want to hear Your voice clearly. When I am confused, realign me so that I am moving in sync with You. I want only Your direction for my life because I want to do Your will. Give me Your guidance please. In Christ, amen.

> "Learning to walk or live in the power
> of the Holy Spirit is the key to victory
> over sin and temptation."

42

A PRAYER FOR A HEART OF GRATITUDE

Lord, help me to be a grateful man and not a complaining man. Help me to see the wonderful things that You've done for me and through me. Help me to recognize what I should be grateful for. May I forever and always show my gratitude by looking for Your goodness in all things. You have given me so much that it's often taken for granted. Sometimes I don't recognize Your good gifts until I'm faced with bad or negative things. This makes it easier for me to grumble rather than give thanks.

Forgive me for my complaining spirit when I have one. And, Lord, while I want to be honest with You about what I see and feel, I don't want to come to You only in the times when life goes wrong. Though I want to have an honest relationship with you where I can be open about my raw emotions, I don't want to be like the Israelites when they were in the wilderness, complaining incessantly at what they saw as challenges rather than opportunities.

Lord, help me to be a grateful man. I want to be thankful for all that You have given to me and to those whom I love. Allow me to experience more of Your blessings to be thankful for—may I not miss even the little things You bring my way. May I not overlook the everydayness of Your faithfulness. Your mercies are new every morning, and for that I am filled with gratitude. In Christ, amen.

> "It's only as we view life as the gift of God that we begin to find its purpose."

43

A PRAYER FOR GOD'S WILL

Lord, You proclaim in Your Word that You reveal Your will to those who are willing to do it. Every day that I get up, would Your Holy Spirit remind me to submit to Your will? Help me to earnestly seek and fully know Your will for my life, and to do so without attempting to negotiate any of it.

May I express complete submission to Your will even before I know how You plan to carry it out. And may I continue to submit to it when I see how You are moving forward. May Your will be so dominant in my thinking, my desires, and my priorities that I cannot escape it. Let my heart seek Your will above all else. And then, based on what You do and how You lead me by the Holy Spirit, may I fully yield to Your guidance, even if I don't understand or am confused by it.

Father, Your will is paramount to me, and I want to carry it out well. I want to honor You with my obedience rather than lapse into resistance and faithlessness. Make me a man who does not argue with You, but instead trusts You in every step that I take. Father, I thank You for showing me Your will because that's what I want to do as Your kingdom man. In Christ, amen.

> "God's ways are not our ways. Yet within the constancy of their change remains one element that never changes, and that is that God is looking for men of faith."

44

A PRAYER FOR FACING TRIALS

Lord, give me the ability to dignify my trials. Whatever You have chosen to send my way, help me to yield to it. Enable me to let that trial carry out the purpose for which You sent it. Open up my heart so that I can hear Your Holy Spirit teach me what You want me to learn. Remind me, Lord, to count it all joy when I run into a trial rather than to complain about it.

Help me look at trials through Your eyes and not through my circumstances or my emotions. Help me to believe what Your Word says in James chapter 1, where You make it clear that trials are for a purpose, and that if we would only ask, You will gladly provide the wisdom we need for dealing with them. Remind me to pray for that wisdom so that when I face the challenges of life I can do so in full reliance upon You.

Give me the power to choose joy even when happiness is not in the midst of the circumstances I'm facing. I want to grow and learn, God. I want to be a man who learns everything You desire for me to learn. Whenever You allow things to happen to me that I don't like, remind me that You have approved those things because You have reason for letting me experience them. Lord, I want to be a man who dignifies my trials by allowing Your divine purpose to be carried out. In Christ, amen.

"God knows where He's taking you. And He knows the lessons you need to know in order to be equipped when you get there."

45

A PRAYER FOR GOD'S GLORY

Lord, manifest Your glory to me. Let me feel the full weight and the impact of Your presence in my life, thoughts, and actions. May the gap between me and You close up more and more so that I am able to walk with a greater sense of your mightiness and strength. Let the atmosphere be more electric around me because of Your consuming of me. Be the fire that burns away unrighteousness and that illuminates Your glory as You did with Moses on the mountain. Your glory was so visible with Moses that others could see it radiate from him. I want to be that man. I want others to experience You more fully when they are in my presence because Your glory rests on me so heavily. Let Your glory surround me always.

Lord, may Your glory shine through me. Let me be a person who exudes Your manifold presence through my life. I don't want to merely talk about it or say how great You are; I want it to be my experience. I want it to be an authentic extension of myself so that anyone who gets close to me will run into Your glory. Make me a man who radiates Your glory because I am consumed by that same glory. In Christ, amen.

> "The closer you get to Jesus, the closer you are to experiencing and fulfilling what you were created to do."

46

A PRAYER FOR EXPANDING MY BOUNDARIES

Lord, show me the boundaries You want me to operate within in my life. Keep me from going outside of the limits that You have prescribed for me so that I don't live in a constant state of frustration. I also don't want to pursue goals that did not originate in Your leading, for Your power and Your presence will not be in those pursuits, which would lead only to difficulties and unfruitfulness. When my choices do not align with Your design and will for me, I am chasing after the wind.

Help me to know the limits of Your calling on my life, my giftedness, and the scope of influence You want me to have. At the same time, may I not be satisfied with where I am at. Maximize my life to the full extent of the boundaries You have set for me. May I not restrict myself out of fear, inactivity, or laziness. Instead, may I reach the far ends of all that You have prescribed for me so that nothing is left undone when my time comes to enter heaven. May I finish my course and complete all that You've called me to do. Enable me to recognize Your calling to the uttermost, Lord, so that I do all You have created me to live out. In Christ, amen.

> "If we are going to put away the excuses that stand between us as we are and the men God wants us to be, we must be men of vision. We must see beyond the ordinary, the everyday, the expected. We must not settle for what's routine or safe."

47

A PRAYER FOR UNDERSTANDING MY IDENTITY

Lord, would You help me to understand my value? Help me to see my worth in Christ. Make me realize how much You love me and how significant I am to You. I admit that there are times when I don't see or feel that value. I don't recognize the worth You have given to me. I'm sure that is my own fault. Maybe it's because of how I am choosing to look at myself. Or maybe it's because I let the people and things around me determine my value. I compare myself to others on social media or at work. This is never good, Lord, because it takes my eyes off of You and I forget my worth to You.

If I would remember how You look at me, love me, leap over me—and that I'm the apple of Your eye—I would rest in the security of my value. If I could see how You see me, then I would be reminded of my true value. God, I don't want to think more of myself than I ought, but I also don't want to think less of myself. I want to think what You think. Show me Your thoughts about me so that I can think those thoughts too. For then I will be the real man you want me to be, and not a fake man looking to fake things or fake people to give me a fake and a wrong definition of who I am. You are my identity, and I want Your identity alone to determine how I view myself. In Christ, amen.

> "God honors a humble heart. He exalts those who have been brought low."

48

A PRAYER FOR DIRECTION

Lord, it is so easy to make wrong decisions. Many times when I am at a crossroad, I don't know which way to go. And sometimes I don't even see the roads clearly. So I give You the right to enter my world and to tell me what You want. May I trust the illumination of the Holy Spirit and obey Your written Word, which gives me all the wisdom I need for the decisions I have to make each and every day.

Lord, I'm not smart enough to make these decisions on my own. And You know that I've made too many dumb ones. I recognize that I have a finite mind, and that affects the choices I make. Your wisdom is infinite, and I want to be able to say, like Jesus, that I did what You wanted me to do. Jesus said in John 17 that He did Your will. I also want to do Your will. I want You to lead me in all that I do. As Psalm 119:105 says, "Your word is a lamp to my feet and a light to my path."

Lord, point me in the direction You want me to take so that I will do what You say to do. May my ears and heart be alert to Your guidance so that I can walk in Your will, according to Your Word. Thank You for directing me personally. In Christ, amen.

> "God may lead you one way in a situation and a totally different way in another very similar situation."

49

A PRAYER FOR PROTECTION

Lord, there are so many dangers in the world in which we live. There are dangerous people doing dangerous things. Sometimes I'm even a danger to myself when I become inattentive or distracted or eat unhealthily or don't manage my stress levels well. So I pray for protection and safety on all fronts. Put a hedge around me so that the evil one doesn't have his way with me. I know that Satan wants to trip me up. I see him coming after my thoughts, actions, relationships, and more. It seems like when I get victory in one area of my life, problems crop up quickly in other areas.

I need Your protection, Lord. I need heaven's helping hand. I need divine intervention to guard me in all that I do. God, shield me from anything that would hurt me—including the evil one, who wants only to destroy me. I see and know that. He's had ample opportunities to do so, and sometimes, in my own foolishness, I've helped him. I don't want to do that anymore. Instead, I want to flee from him and draw closer to You. Please protect me as I follow You by covering me with Christ's blood and surrounding me with Your angels—Your sentry—every step I take. In Christ, amen.

> "Once you realize that you are in a spiritual battle with the forces of evil, you will become very sensitive to sin's attempts to conquer you. In a war, only a fool is not on constant alert for the enemy."

50

A PRAYER FOR THE PROTECTION OF MY LOVED ONES

Lord, would You protect my loved ones? Would You shield my siblings along with my immediate family? Those who are close to me, Lord, would You safeguard them? Protect them from physical and emotional danger. Keep them safe from satanic and demonic affliction. Lord, without Your protection, we're at the mercy of the world and the evil one. We're at the whim of the unrighteous. Throughout the Psalms, David asked for Your protection. I join him in asking for the same, Father. I plead for You to

cover my children and loved ones with Christ's cove-
nantal care and surround them all with Your spiritual
warriors. Protect them from those peers who would
lead them into drugs, immorality, evil, and other
wrong things. Shield them from the vices that would
seek to suck them downward and destroy their lives.

Shelter my loved ones, Lord; they need Your protection. I can't always be there for them, and even
when I am, I still appeal to Your power to defend
them from anything that would destroy them. So,
Father, protect those whom I love because You love
them too. In Christ, amen.

> "Nehemiah didn't ignore the threats made
> against him or pretend they weren't real. He
> prayed for God's protection, but he also put
> his faith into action."

51

A PRAYER FOR STRENGTHENING MY RELATIONSHIP WITH GOD

Lord, I have decisions to make, and I don't want to make the wrong ones. Would You show me the right choices so that I can honor You in what I decide to do?

Please start with the decisions I need to make about me—which includes my personal walk with You. Help me to make good choices about the amount of time I spend in prayer and reading my Bible. There are also times when I go too long without praising You. Convict me of all this and have

Your Spirit say to me, "You haven't talked with Me for a while. Let's talk."

God, please don't allow me to get used to not having a personal time with You or unveiling my soul to You. May I be intentional about coming to You, Lord. May I not approach You with generalities and vagueness that reveal a lack of earnestness about communicating with You. I want to come to You with complete transparency, to let You know my specific thoughts, struggles, and doubts. I want to commit myself to talking with You more regularly so that You can meet me where I am and heal me where I am.

As for the decisions I need to make that go beyond me, provide clarity of mind for me so that I make wise and informed choices. I want to do what is right the first time around, and I want to be corrected when I do what is wrong. Help me to exercise discipline so I don't make the wrong choices over and over again. Thank You that as You correct me, You also show Your mercy. May I be earnest in staying connected with You so that I remain in the place of blessing. In Christ, amen.

"Without Jesus, we would have no chance of understanding God. To understand and know Jesus is to understand and know God."

52

A PRAYER FOR GOD'S FAVOR

Lord, will You give me Your favor? May I live under the cover of Your blessing? Deuteronomy 29 says that Your covenant gives blessing. I want to live in Your favor and in Your good graces.

Lord, when I'm walking away from Your favor, when I'm leaving the tent, when I'm going into the world, when I'm abandoning Your way and Your will and Your Word, make me so unhappy and so uncomfortable that I run back into the covering of Your favor. Cause me to return to the covenant of blessing.

Father, may I be able to say that one day in Your

house, in Your favor, is more delight to me than a thousand days somewhere else. One day with You is better than a million years without You. I've lived too many days without Your favor, and the price tag has been high. I don't want to pay that price any longer. I want the rest of my life to be lived in Your favor—so that when I'm going through a rough time, I still know and feel the abundance of Your presence.

Lord, grant me Your favor. In Christ, amen.

> "The basic definition of God's grace is His undeserved favor to us. It is God doing for us what we could never do for ourselves."

53

A PRAYER FOR THE GIFT OF ENCOURAGEMENT

Lord, may the value that You have placed upon each member of my family be the value that I place upon them as well. May You give me a word to say every day that expresses how I value my wife and my children. May they know that they matter to me not because of some general sense of "I love you," but because of specific words and actions that demonstrate my love. Use my words to minister grace to the hearer—I want to be a grace minister in my home.

I want to see my wife and children smile every

time I'm approaching them because they know I'm going to compliment them, say an encouraging word, or pray a blessing over them. I dedicate my family to You, Lord, in how I treat them. May I always speak well of their accomplishments and may I encourage them even while I correct their failures. May my every interaction with them be carried out in a spirit of love.

Lord, give me this attitude and spirit of love so that it will consume me as I minister to my loved ones. I truly want them to know that I cherish them and live to do so. Thank You for the Spirit's reminder for me to live in this way. In Christ, amen.

> "Your children need the right information and the right application. You can't leave them to themselves and expect someone else to teach and encourage them. This is on you."

54

A PRAYER FOR MOVING BEYOND MY PAST

Lord, I have some regrets in my yesterdays. When I look to the past and some of the things I have done, I am disappointed in myself. I'm seeking Your forgiveness for certain thoughts, actions, and perspectives that didn't honor You. Lord, I don't want to be incarcerated by my past mistakes. I don't want yesterday to own me because when it does, it ruins my today and even undermines my hope for tomorrow.

Help me to get past my failures, but help me to learn from them too. May I use them as a rearview mirror to see what yesterday was like and how I want to avoid repeating that. More importantly, may I look ahead through the windshield of where You're taking me and where You want me to go. Help me to use the lessons of the past so that I live more wisely in the future, in a way that brings honor to You.

Lord, may I also benefit from the successes of yesterday—from the things that I did right. Help me to build on those so that I have a better tomorrow. At the same time, help me to not be locked into yesterday's accomplishments as though You have nothing new and exciting for me tomorrow. Lord, may I look forward to my tomorrows knowing that You love to bless—and keep blessing—those who belong to You. In Christ, amen.

> "The first step to overcoming the past is realizing that no matter what others do to you, if the Lord is with you, that is truly all you need."

55

A PRAYER FOR LETTING GO OF SHAME

Lord, I'm holding on to some things that I'm having trouble letting go of. I feel glued to them. When I look back at some of what I've said and done— some of my regrets—it's hard to let go. The bell still rings about the sounds that I made. The hurt that I inflicted and the pain that I brought upon myself and others still brings guilt and shame. I'm asking Your forgiveness for those things because I realize that when I hurt others, I also hurt You. That's what sin does—it hurts You. I am so sorry, Father. I thank

You for the cross, for Christ shedding His blood to pay for my sins and make forgiveness possible.

May Your Spirit help me let go emotionally of what I've let go spiritually. I've confessed my sins to You, Lord—I've named them to You, and You've promised that You will not remember them. Thank You for that. Now I need You to help me forget them as well. Enable me to let go of them so that I can move forward in a way that gives You glory and honor. Thank You that I can celebrate the fact that You have forgiven my sins and will remember them no more. In Christ, amen.

"Regardless of what happened yesterday, if you will stick with the Lord today, your yesterday won't control your tomorrow."

56

A PRAYER FOR RESTING IN THE LORD

Lord, bring calm to my soul. Help me to rest in You. You told me in Matthew 11:28-29 that if I come to You and yoke myself with You, that You would give me rest. I need that, Lord. Everywhere I look, there is turmoil—in my own heart, in my family, and in society. I look at the news and it's depressing. I hear conversations at work and they are discouraging. God, I need to know the tranquility You alone can bring to my soul.

I need to be at home and calm on the inside—in my spirit—despite the chaos that I can't control on the outside. Lord, give me the ability to relax in You, to be comfortable in You, and to be trustful of You. To believe You even when I don't understand You. And to verify and validate that trust by my praise of You. Help me to say, even when I'm down, what David said in Psalm 42 about running after You like the deer who pants for the water brooks. Enable me to say that I will yet trust in You even though I don't see You right now. I want to know how to wait on You, trust in You, believe in You, and acknowledge that You are in control. In Christ, amen.

> "Even God rested from His work of creation on the seventh day (see Genesis 2:1-3). To enjoy His accomplishments, He stepped back and looked at them. He was finished, so He rested. Now God didn't rest because He was tired. His rest was the rest of accomplishment, of a job well done. It was the rest of reflection on and enjoyment of His work."

57

A PRAYER FOR ALIGNING MYSELF UNDER GOD

Lord, I'm often distracted and pulled away from what I should be focused on. Help me to see my moments and days through Your eyes. I want the glasses of the Spirit of God to help me see clearly and put first things first. My walk with You needs to be a greater priority. My choices before You need to reflect Your overarching rule in my life. My wife and my family need to be focused on You in their decisions as well.

Help me to align myself under You so that my

focus is what it should be. Help me to be kingdom-minded in my perspective. Keep me from distractions that would pull me away and cause me to pay too much attention to matters that are of lower priority. May I make time for what should come first. Not half of my time, not makeup time, not last-minute time, but time that makes it clear You matter to me most.

God, as I call on You, as I cry to You, keep me focused on the main things so that my personal life and my family life don't go lacking because I've put other things in their place. Give me Your priorities and help me by reminding me that they should be mine as well. In Christ, amen.

> "God's definition of a kingdom man is a man who operates all of his life underneath the overarching rule of God."

58

A PRAYER FOR FULFILLING GOD'S PURPOSE FOR ME

Lord, You said in Acts 13:36 that David served Your purposes for his generation. That's what I want to do as well. I want to serve Your purposes, not my own. I want to do what You want, and to do it the way You want it done.

Lord, show me Your purpose. Show me Your divine design for how You want to use my gifts, talents, personality, and experiences to advance Your kingdom and to bring good to others. May I make myself wholly available to You so that You can do Your work through me unhindered.

I want to fulfill Your kingdom purpose for my life. I don't want to just go to work, come home, and watch television or surf the Internet and do nothing that has an eternal benefit. I want to be a man of destiny, a man who uses his spiritual giftedness to make a difference in the lives of others. Give me Your vision for my life so that I can act on it and obey it. Thank You for showing me Your purpose for me. In Christ, amen.

> "It's true that if you aim at nothing, you'll hit it every time. If you want meaning and purpose, you need to have a goal, something to reach for. You need to have a vision."

59

A PRAYER FOR MY LOVED ONES TO FIND GOD'S PURPOSE FOR THEM

Lord, I know one of the purposes You've given me is to guide my family to their purpose, and that means that I need to understand clearly what You want done with my family. I'm going to start with Your Word, and I'm going to expose myself to what You are insisting that I do as the head of my home.

As I do that, help me to see the uniqueness of my wife and each of my children—to see their talents and skills so that I can help guide them to their purpose. I want to fulfill my responsibility to encourage them to seek Your purpose for their lives. Help me to see what You see in each loved one You've placed in my care and to train up each one according to their bent, the unique way You've created them. Enable me to recognize how You have gifted each one of them.

Lord, help me to guide my family right so that they are living in Your will and not merely existing. I want them to sense that they are living according to Your design for them, and that I'm leading them there. That "follow the leader" means we're going somewhere. That we're all growing toward You, but each in our own unique way. Help me to see how You are going to use each person for You and the benefit of each other within our home. Give me insight on how to point my loved ones first and foremost toward You. In Christ, amen.

> "If you want to find your purpose, don't go looking for it. Look for the Purpose-giver."

60

A PRAYER FOR SPIRITUAL SENSITIVITY

Lord, I want to serve others better. I want our community to benefit from what I have to offer. There are so many different ways I could serve for the benefit of our community. Help me to be sensitive to where the Spirit is leading me. Point me to the people that You want me to reach, and to the entities You want me to be involved with. Help me with wisdom so that I don't waste my time, my life, my gifts, or my efforts. But I also don't want to be selfish.

You told me that I'm to love others starting with

my family, then the body of Christ, then my community. May everything I do contribute toward a wholesome, healthy, safe, and productive family, church, and society. Show me where I can make the best use of my limited time. Reveal to me where I should invest myself for the maximum benefit that You want to produce through me. After I've taken the time to meet the needs of my family, show me who You want me to minister to next. I know that Jesus didn't serve at random. You led Him where You wanted Him to go. Lead me, Lord, and I'll go where You want me to—all because I desire to follow You. Make me a wise steward of the time and talents You have given me. In Christ, amen.

"A steward owns nothing, but he manages everything. When a steward starts acting like he owns his master's stuff, there are problems (see Luke 16:1-2). The Bible declares that God owns it all, even you."

61

A PRAYER FOR BALANCE IN MY LIFE

Lord, help me keep a healthy balance between my responsibilities on the job and at home. May I not neglect either. May I serve You with excellence in employment without compromising or downgrading my service to You in my family.

Help me to see my family as a joy and not a drudgery, and to be diligent about meeting their needs. And in my workplace, equip me to be productive and make progress. I don't want to be a slouch in either place, which means I need You to help me to balance what I do and how I do it. May I be willing to give up some of my entertainment time, and yes, even my sports time if it means my wife or kids need me. Help me not to be so engrossed in myself that my job or my family goes lacking.

At the same time, please help my family to understand when it's necessary for me to do extra things so I can keep providing for them. As I'm investing in them, may they invest back in me so that my work does not suffer. It can be a tough balancing act, Lord, but with Your Spirit and Your guidance, I can do both well. I'm leaning on You to help me do what is right and best for my family and my job.

Would You help me with my work boundaries? I realize my job is what enables me to care for the needs of my family, but I don't want to become so addicted to my work that I use it as an excuse for neglecting my role as a husband and father. Help me to be willing to earn less of an income if that is what is necessary to be a good man at home. And provide me the kind of work environment that enhances my ability to fulfill my role at home. I ask this because I want to be a good father and a good husband as well as a good employee. In Christ, amen.

"Your work can become a source of sin
when God's will is excluded. Conversely,
it becomes blessed when God's
will is included."

62

A PRAYER FOR MY JOB

Lord, You talk a lot in Your Word about the manner in which I am to serve at my job. You say that I am to work as though I'm doing it for You. Sometimes that's not easy—too often I fail to see my job as a service to You. Please help me to maintain a right perspective. May Your Holy Spirit remind me that everything I do is to be done as though I'm working for You.

Help me to see the spiritual nature of my work and not just the tasks themselves. May I recognize my job is yet another way I can fulfill Your divine calling for my life. And give me the sensitivity to minister to others in ways that are appropriate. Help me to see the people around me as individuals whom I can witness to, encourage, and build up. May I never hesitate to live out Your purpose for me in the workplace.

Thank You as well for the ways You provide for me and my family through my job. May my gratitude be on display in the attitude that I have in the workplace. I want to see that side of my life through Your eyes so that I am mindful of what You want me to do. Every time I go to my work, may I see You in all the tasks I do. I want to view my job as both a divine responsibility to You and an obligation to my employer.

Thank You, Lord, for my job. Help me to carry it out well in accordance with Your purpose. In Christ, amen.

> "You can have the best job in the world and still be empty inside because work in and of itself can't give you meaning. You need a purpose."

63

A PRAYER FOR SUCCESS ON MY JOB

Lord, would You enable me to be successful at my job? By that I mean massively productive. I don't want to do just enough to get by. I want to do outstanding work for You because You deserve excellence. I want to give my best. I want to blow other people's minds over how well I do my work and how productive I am.

Will You do for me like You did with Joseph and Potiphar, and give me great success in the eyes of those whom I work for? I pray for the kind of success that is visible—the kind that Potiphar saw, and that my employer will see. Help them to notice my productivity not because I'm bragging about it, but because You've made it visible in the integrity, character, and quality of what I do. Let me do well so that the results of my labor are obvious to all.

And then, Lord, please reward me for the work that I do. Reward me financially, reward me with recognition—not in a prideful way, but humble. I want others to know that I take my job seriously. I recall how, in Daniel 6, some officials tried to accuse Daniel but were unable to find anything wrong with him and his work. May people find nothing wrong with my labors both on the job and for Your kingdom. Give me a vision for what You want to accomplish through me so that You receive glory and honor. In Christ, amen.

> "Destiny produces a sense of vision and a willingness to dream dreams to get there. A visionless man is a man with little or no sense of calling."

64

A PRAYER FOR UNITY

Lord, in the world in which we live, our communities are decaying. May I not simply be a complainer about this, but rather, a healer who offers solutions. May my involvement in my community demonstrate Christlikeness. May I follow in Christ's footsteps and bring help to others as He did. May I bring unity where there is division. May I actively condemn wrong and promote what is right.

May my presence in my community be wholesome and uplifting and strengthening so that others are inspired to make positive contributions as well. May my family have that kind of influence too. May we all serve in ways that build bridges that cross racial, denominational, social, and cultural lines. May our neighborhood not simply be a place where we live, but where we are involved and are a powerful force for change. May our presence make a real difference for unity among people, and may we make time to do the things that will forge oneness.

Give me wisdom on how to best use my time, and our family time, for the well-being, stability, harmony, and improvement of the community that I seek to serve. In Christ, amen.

> "Committed Christians are also 'peacemakers.' They pursue unity, not divisiveness. They seek to pull people together, not tear them apart."

65

A PRAYER FOR BUILDING UP OTHERS

Lord, I know that You have a heart for discipleship. I know that You want us to invest in the lives of others and have others invest in us. Show me who You want me to mentor. Reveal to me who I can look to as an example so that as I'm poured into, I also pour out to others.

Father, keep me from becoming a cul-de-sac that seeks only what is good for me, rather than living as a conduit through which blessings can flow through me to others. I know that Your definition of a blessing is not only what flows to me, but also what flows through me. May I be a vehicle, a channel, a tool that You can use to help other people, particularly other men, grow in their faith, commitment, and leadership.

May I make time to invest in others. Help me to avoid the trap of watching out only for myself. I want the spiritual riches that You give to me to be handed on to others—so that when it's all said and done, others have been encouraged by my growth as well as their own. You give so that we might give to others. May I be generous as I disciple others and receive the guidance others give me. In Christ, amen.

"If you want to be a man who has an impact, you don't start with political or social or economic solutions, although all three of these eventually came into play in Nehemiah's case. Rather, you fall before God in fasting and prayer, and you go to the Word."

66

A PRAYER FOR USING THE GIFTS I'VE BEEN GIVEN

Lord, You made it clear in Your Word that You've given every believer spiritual gifts. You've given each of us divine enablements for the purpose of serving You and others. Please make it clear what my gifts are so that I'm not just going through the motions, but I'm fulfilling my purpose through the use of my gifts. Make it so that I'm not merely busy, but I am on target with the time and the talents that You have put on loan to me.

Lord, I don't want to waste my life. I want to

invest in Your kingdom. And that means I need to know clearly how to put my gifts to use so that the Holy Spirit can take me to the next level of my spiritual growth in You. Father, I want to know the gifts, to see them, to understand them, to develop them, and to utilize them for Your glory and the good of others. I realize that there is coming a day when You will reward me for how my gifts were used. May I be diligent, then, in putting those enablements to use. Thank You that, as I exercise good stewardship of Your gifts, I will discover the power of contentment in all that I do. In Christ, amen.

> "One reward for faithful stewardship is contentment, a quality of life so elusive that the world has been chasing it for centuries and still hasn't found it."

67

A PRAYER FOR A BIGGER VISION

Lord, help me to look further than I can see. I want to be a man of faith, a man with vision. Help me not to be like the king who didn't shoot all his arrows out the window. I want to shoot all my arrows. I want to see all that heaven wants to accomplish in me, for me, to me, and through me in my life, for my family, for my church, and for the community and world in which I live.

Help me to see what You see for me and not be limited to my finite vision. But also help me to have the right vision—I don't want to think big or see big with the wrong motives. Help me to keep Your glory in mind as You show me what You want for my life. As I spend time in Your presence, make Your vision for my life clear so that I do not waste time dreaming wrong dreams that will become nightmares because they weren't Your desires for me. Dream through me. May Your Holy Spirit put Your thoughts in my mind so that I am dreaming Your dreams and not merely my own. I want to have Your perspective for my life. In Christ, amen.

> "Pursuing a vision always involves taking some risks. You must be willing to step out in faith and dependence on God."

68

A PRAYER FOR ABIDING WITH CHRIST

Lord, I know that what I want from You comes from intimacy with You. And yet I find myself neglecting Jesus far too often. I don't abide with Him enough. Instead, I abide in my favorite TV shows, the news, social media, and so many other distractions. I stay caught up on all of that, but when it comes to spending time with Jesus, I barely take time to visit. I don't hang out with my Savior.

Jesus, I recognize the need to include You in all of my life. This means I need to hang out more with You. It's only as I interface with You and spend time with You that I'll see You at work in my life. You are my king, and I want to be Your kingdom man. Help me to know You more. May I wholeheartedly yield to Your authority. May I be more in tune with You. I want to be on the same wavelength as you so that I am hearing from You, experiencing You, and growing in You. Help me to realize more of Your work in my life.

Lord, in the times when I've forgotten You, speak to me through Your Spirit. Pinprick my heart and bring conviction when we need some more time together. I want to grow closer to You, and that means making You a priority. In Christ, amen.

> "Pursue Christ as a Person you are in love with, and you will find the grace of God giving you power to pull off the program of God."

69

A PRAYER FOR MY MARRIAGE

Lord, I pray for my marriage. As I do so, I realize that means praying first and foremost for my wife. I ask that You would guard her, guide her, and protect her. At the same time, may I be intentional about paying attention to her needs, wants, and desires. Help me to make our marriage not just about me and my dreams and the ways that my wife can help me. Instead, may she sense that every decision I make takes her into consideration. May it be evident that I have her best interests in mind. Lord, may I never become so prideful that I fail to seek her advice, suggestions, thoughts, and warnings.

God, may I let her know that what she thinks and says matters immensely to me. May she never feel ignored or marginalized because I've got time for everybody and everything else. Help me to search for ways that I can invest in her interests, and may I genuinely support what You have called her to do and help her make that happen. I don't want to be the kind of husband who demands that she set her dreams and goals aside for my sake. Help me to stay focused on her, Lord, and not insist that she stay focused on me. Help me to make our marriage relationship a place of equality and enjoyment. Let love lead everything we do, and let grace season every word we say. In Christ, amen.

> "You cannot leave God at the altar and expect to have a happy marriage."

More Great Harvest House Books
by Dr. Tony Evans

30 Days to Overcoming Addictive Behavior

30 Days to Overcoming Emotional Strongholds

30 Days to Victory Through Forgiveness

Discover Your Destiny

Experience the Power of God's Names

Horizontal Jesus

Horizontal Jesus Study Guide

It's Not Too Late

A Moment for Your Soul (eBook only)

The Power of God's Names

Prayers for Victory in Spiritual Warfare

Prayers for Victory in Your Marriage

Praying Through the Names of God

Victory in Spiritual Warfare

Watch Your Mouth

Watch Your Mouth DVD

Watch Your Mouth Growth and Study Guide

Watch Your Mouth Interactive Workbook

Your Comeback

Your Comeback DVD

Your Comeback Interactive Workbook

To learn more about Harvest House books and
to read sample chapters, visit our website:

www.harvesthousepublishers.com

HARVEST HOUSE PUBLISHERS
EUGENE, OREGON